D1225090

MAR 1 6

GREAT ENGINEERING

BUILDING
DIKES and
LEVEES

REBECCA STEFOFF

Cavendish
Square

New York

Published in 2016 by Cavendish Square Publishing, LLC
243 5th Avenue, Suite 136, New York, NY 10016

Website: cavendishsq.com

This publication represents the opinions and views of the author based on his or her personal experience, knowledge, and research. The information in this book serves as a general guide only. The author and publisher have used their best efforts in preparing this book and disclaim liability rising directly or indirectly from the use and application of this book.

CPSIA Compliance Information: Batch #WS15CSQ

All websites were available and accurate when this book was sent to press.

Library of Congress Cataloging-in-Publication Data

Stefoff, Rebecca, 1951-
Building dikes and levees / Rebecca Stefoff.
pages cm
Includes bibliographical references and index.
ISBN 978-1-50260-610-5 (hardcover) ISBN 978-1-50260-609-9 (paperback) ISBN 978-1-50260-611-2 (ebook)
1. Dikes (Engineering) 2. Levees. I. Title.

TC337.S74 2016
627'.42—dc23

2015006645

Editorial Director: David McNamara
Editor: Andrew Coddington
Copy Editor: Rebecca Rohan
Art Director: Jeffrey Talbot
Designer: Amy Greenan
Senior Production Manager: Jennifer Ryder-Talbot
Production Editor: Renni Johnson
Photo Research: J8 Media

The photographs in this book are used by permission and through the courtesy of: Bas Meelker/Shutterstock.com, cover; Alfredo Estrella/AFP/Getty Images, 5; Zacarias Pereira da Sandeen/File:Natural levees.png/Wikimedia Commons, 9; E R Degginger/Science Source/Getty Images, 11; The Sacramento Bee, Randall Benton/AP Images, 12; Goodluz/Shutterstock.com, 14; Corepics VOF/Shutterstock.com, 15; Joe Raedle/Getty Images, 17; Toa55/Shutterstock.com, 18; ZUMA Press, Inc./Alamy, 20; Marc Pinter/Shutterstock.com, 21; Mario Tama/Getty Images, 23; CreativeNature R.Zwerver/Shutterstock.com, 27.

Printed in the United States of America

TABLE OF CONTENTS

CHAPTER **ONE**

Fighting Floods

Water is important. Every animal and plant needs it. But too much water can be a big problem!

Too much water can cause a **flood**. A flood happens when water flows over land that is dry most of the time.

Floods cover land and roads. They ruin houses. They kill the crops growing on farms. Big floods can drown people and animals.

One way to keep floods from happening is to build a **dike** or **levee**.

Rivers in Mexico spilled over their banks to flood this town in 2007.

Dikes and levees are walls that hold water back and keep it from flowing onto the land.

Some levees form without human help. They are built up along the edges of rivers by soil and gravel that wash up onto the banks.

Other levees are built by people to protect the land from floods.

Kinds of Floods

Some floods happen on the ocean coast. A storm pushes high waves onto the land. An earthquake on the bottom of the sea sends huge waves in all directions.

High winds drive huge waves toward the shore. This could cause a flood.

Rain can also cause a flood. If rain falls faster than the ground can soak it up, water sits on top of the ground. A little rain makes puddles. A *lot* of rain may make a flood.

Most floods happen along rivers. If the water in the river rises, the river may flow over its banks. It covers the **floodplain**, the land on both sides of the river that can be flooded.

Why does the water in a river rise? The reason might be heavy rain. The rain runs into the river, and the river carries it downstream. As more water joins the river, the river becomes too big for its banks.

The problem with river floods is that many people live near rivers. A river is a source of water for people and farm crops. It is a highway for boats that carry people and goods. That's why people build homes and cities along rivers. Millions of people are in danger when those rivers flood.

China's River Problem

The people of ancient China knew that rivers can be both helpful and dangerous. They built dikes and levees to tame their rivers.

Some of the first levees were built along the Yellow River in northern China. The Yellow River is 3,400 miles (5,472 kilometers) long. It is the sixth-longest river in the world.

The Yellow River picks up soil in the high lands of western China. Later it drops the soil in the flat lands below. This soil around the river is good for farming. But it also builds up on the bottom of the Yellow River. Over time, the built-up soil lifts the river. Floods happen more often. Almost three thousand years ago, the Chinese people found ways to fight the floods.

The Yellow River in China had some of the world's first levees.

One way was to dig ditches and **canals** to move water out of the river. These human-built waterways carried river water into farm fields.

Another way to fight floods was to build up the banks of the Yellow River. Higher banks kept water from spreading across the land.

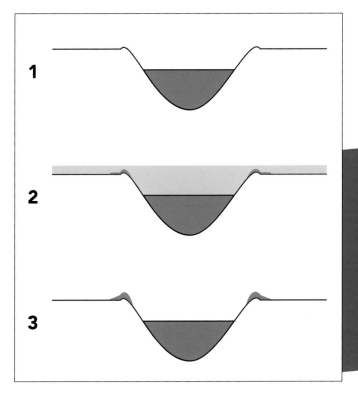

This diagram shows how levees naturally form when a river floods. The water pushes dirt up its banks and leaves a protective rim along the top.

People carried dirt and rocks to the river in wagons and buckets. They piled the dirt and rocks into walls along the river. Then they packed down the walls to make them solid. These levees held the Yellow River in its banks.

Over many years, China built one of the largest networks of levees in the world.

CHAPTER TWO

Walls Against Water

Today many countries use levees to prevent floods. One of those countries is the United States. Levees run for hundreds of miles along the Mississippi River and the Sacramento River.

New dikes and levees are being built in countries around the world. Before a levee can be built, the builders have to make a plan.

A levee on the Mississippi River. Here, the river is higher than the land next to it.

Planning a Dike or Levee

Planning a new dike or levee has several steps.

First, experts have to decide how to solve their water problem. A levee by itself might not be enough. For a big river, flood control might take a mix of levees, canals, and **dams**.

Next, money has to be found to pay for the levee. Most levees are paid for by the government of a

A fisherman tries his luck next to a dam. Dams also control water.

country or a state. The **concrete**, stone, or other material that makes up the levee is just part of the cost. Most of the money that is spent on a levee goes to the people who plan and build it.

The next step is learning about the river. How much water flows through it? How much is the most water that could flow during a flood? How fast does the water move?

The answers to these questions will tell planners how tall the levee has to be to protect the floodplain. They will also tell planners whether the levee should be made out of packed dirt, stone, concrete, steel, or a mix of all four.

A Team Job

It takes a team of experts to plan a levee. Some of them are **engineers**.

Engineers use the tools of math and science to plan and build all kinds of things, from spaceships to the software that runs computers. Engineers who work on big projects for the good of the public, such as dams and levees, are called **civil engineers**.

A **hydrologist** also helps plan the levee. Hydrologists are scientists who study water. They are experts in the **current**, or flow, of moving water. Hydrologists know how hard the current will push against the levee when the amount of water in the river goes up or down.

Scientists must study a river before a levee can be built.

Another member of the team is a **geologist**. This scientist studies the earth. Geologists know how different kinds of soil, such as sand and clay, act when they are wet. They can tell whether the riverbanks are strong enough to hold up the levee.

Making a Blueprint

The last step in planning a levee is making a **blueprint** for the job. A blueprint is a plan that shows every step of the work and where every piece of the levee will go.

The team of experts makes the blueprint. The builders who do the work will follow it carefully. Engineers will usually be in charge of the job to make sure that everything goes as planned.

When the blueprint is ready, it's time to build the levee.

Engineers check their blueprints at every stage of a building project.

CHAPTER THREE

Constructing a Water Barrier

Anything that holds back water can be called a levee. Even a bag full of sand can be used to hold back water.

When it looks like there might be a flood, people pile up sandbags. Sandbags along the edge of a river act like a levee. They help keep the river from overflowing. Sandbags in front of a door soak up floodwater. They help keep the water out of houses and stores.

Fearing a flood, people pile sandbags to make a simple levee.

After the flood danger is over, sandbag walls come down. Other levees are different. They are built to last.

Making a Levee

The oldest levees were made of stones and soil thousands of years ago. Today most levees are still made of stones and soil. But there are some big differences.

A machine called an excavator scoops dirt onto a riverbank.

Engineers today use computers to plan the levees. They use big machines such as dump trucks, bulldozers, and steam shovels. These machines can move tons of rock and earth in a few days.

The first step in making a levee is to prepare the ground. Workers make sure that the place where the levee will stand is flat and level.

The next step is to build the levee. Workers build in layers: first stone, then sand or soil, then more stone, then more soil.

Each new layer is a little smaller than the last layer. The levee slants inward from bottom to top, like a pyramid. Because levees are wider at the bottom than at the top, they are strongest at the bottom. This makes them harder to wash away.

Most levees are flat on top. People can walk along the top of the levee to check it for damage. They can pile sandbags on the flat top in case of high flood.

Protecting Dikes and Levees

Water that is moving washes the land away. This is called **erosion**. If the land is solid rock, erosion by rain, rivers, or ocean waves is slow. If the land is loose soil, erosion happens fast.

Erosion is the biggest problem for levees. A flood can erode a riverbank or a levee overnight. Even the slow day-by-day flow of the river's current can weaken a levee over time.

Sand scraped from the ocean floor is being used to protect a California beach.

Levee builders have ways to protect the levees from erosion. One way is to plant special kinds of grass. The strong roots of the grass make a web in the soil that helps hold the levee together. This is why many levees look like long, grassy hills.

Another way to protect a levee is to use waterproof material. On the side that faces the water, a levee may be covered with concrete, metal, or plastic. Or metal bars may be driven deep into the ground along the levee to help hold the stones and soil in place.

Other Water Barriers

Not all dikes and levees run along riverbanks. In many places, people have built dikes to hold back the water of the oceans. Sometimes these barriers are called sea walls. They protect low-lying land from extra-high waves and storms.

These silver "shells" are gates that can come down to block floodwater from this English river.

CHAPTER FOUR

Do Levees Work?

Dikes and levees do a lot of good around the world. Together with dams and canals, they help people control an important natural resource: water.

For millions of people, levees and dikes are the first line of protection against floods. Sometimes, though, levees fail. What happens then can be a disaster.

Levee Failures

When floodwater fills a river, the river wants to spread out across its floodplain. If a levee keeps the river from

The dirt levee around this house failed when the Mississippi River flooded.

spreading out, all the water stays in the river. This makes the river deeper and faster. The river pushes harder against its banks—and against the levees.

Levees may keep a river from flooding in one place. But downstream from that place, the river is more powerful. It might become strong enough to break through the levees there and cause a flood.

Levees fail in two ways. One way is **overtopping**. This happens when the water in a river rises high enough to spill over the top of the levee.

The other kind of failure is called a **breach**. This is a crack or hole in the levee. A breach can be caused by erosion, or by the force of a lot of fast-moving water, or by logs or other things crashing into the levee. After the first breach, a whole section of the levee may be swept away.

Breaches are worse than overtoppings. When a river overtops its levee, there is a flood, but the levee is still there when the water level in the river begins to go down. The flood may not last a long time, and only some of the water will flow onto the land.

When a levee is breached, there is no wall of protection. Much of the river may pour out through the broken wall. This kind of flood can last for a long time. And when the floodwaters disappear, the levee must be repaired or replaced.

Historic Floods

Levee failures have caused huge floods. In 1887, heavy rain filled China's Yellow River to the bursting point. The river broke through dikes in northern China and flooded an area as large as the state of Alabama. More than a million people died. Two million were left homeless.

In 2005, a hurricane named Katrina swept through the American city of New Orleans. The city sits on the Mississippi River. Much of the city lies below the river level, protected by dikes and levees.

Katrina drove high water and winds against the dikes and levees of New Orleans. Some were overtopped. More than sixty were breached. Much of the city was flooded. Water stood 10 feet (3 meters) deep in some places.

Engineers learn from each levee disaster. Their goal is to build better water barriers for the future. Some of the world's best builders of dikes and levees are the Dutch. Their country, the Netherlands, has a long history of building walls against water.

The Dutch Make New Land

The Netherlands is a small, mostly flat country in Europe. It is bordered by the North Sea. For hundreds of years the Dutch people have built dikes and sea walls to protect their low-lying country from storms and waves.

The Dutch did not use dikes just for protection from a stormy sea. They used them to make new land.

As early as five hundred years ago, the Dutch started to drain lakes and ponds. First they built dikes around the lakes. Then they used the power of windmills to pump the water out of the lakes. The lakes were turned into dry land for farms and towns.

The Dutch have used dikes and windmills to drain water out of lakes and rivers, leaving pieces of land called polders.

Pieces of land that were drained this way are called **polders**. The Netherlands has three thousand of them! Each polder is surrounded by dikes that keep water from filling it up again.

Other countries have polders, too. They are just one of the ways that people use dikes and levees. As long as people live near the ocean and along rivers, they will need these walls to hold back the raging waters.

GLOSSARY

blueprint A detailed plan for building something, showing every step and every part.

breach A hole, crack, or other break.

canal A human-made ditch, channel, or river.

civil engineer An engineer who makes bridges, dams, roads, and other structures for the public to use.

concrete A blend of sand, gravel, cement, and water that is hard and strong when it dries.

current The flow of water, or the speed at which the water is moving.

dam A barrier that keeps water from flowing freely.

dike A wall or barrier against high water and floods; a levee.

engineer Someone who uses science to plan and build things.

erosion The action of water that washes away land.

flood An overflow of water onto dry land.

floodplain An area of low ground, near a river or other body of water, that could be flooded.

geologist A scientist who studies geology, the subject of the earth and what it is made of.

hydrologist A scientist who studies water and the movement of water.

levee A wall or barrier against high water or floods, usually along the banks of a river; a dike.

overtopping When water rises high enough to spill over the top of a dike or levee.

polder A low-lying piece of land that is surrounded by dikes to keep out water.

FIND OUT MORE

Books

Latham, Donna. *Canals and Dams: Investigate Feats of Engineering*. White River Junction, VT: Nomad Press, 2013.

Mattern, Joanne. *Floods, Dams, and Levees*. Vero Beach, FL: Rourke Publishing Group, 2011.

Murray, Peter. *Forces of Nature: Floods*. North Mankato, MN: Childs World, 2015.

Websites

Dikes of the Netherlands

science.howstuffworks.com/engineering/structural/levee2.htm

National Geographic Education: Levee

education.nationalgeographic.com/education/encyclopedia/levee/?ar_a=1

INDEX

Page numbers in **boldface** are illustrations. Entries in **boldface** are glossary terms.

ABOUT THE AUTHOR

Rebecca Stefoff has written books for young readers on many topics in science, technology, and history. She is the author of the six-volume series Is It Science? (Cavendish Square, 2014) and the four-volume series Animal Behavior Revealed (Cavendish Square, 2014). She also wrote *The Telephone*, *The Camera*, *Submarines*, *The Microscope and Telescope*, and *Robots* for Cavendish Square's Great Inventions series. Stefoff lives in Portland, Oregon. You can learn more about Stefoff and her books for young people at www.rebeccastefoff.com.